The Essential Network:

Success Through Personal Connections

John L. Bennett

The Essential Network:

Success Through Personal Connections

John L. Bennett

Mooresville, North Carolina

Copyright 2001. All Rights Reserved.

The Essential Network: Success Through Connections

Copyright 2001 by John L. Bennett

All rights reserved. No part of this book may be reproduced or transmitted in any form or by any means, electronic or mechanical, including photocopying, recording, or by any information storage and retrieval system, without permission in writing from the publisher.

This publication is designed to provide accurate and authoritative information in regard to the subject matter covered. It is sold with the understanding that the publisher is not engaged in rendering professional services. If professional advice or other expert assistance is required, the services of a competent professional person should be sought. This book is printed on acid-free paper.

Art Direction & Design
Eric Johnson, Twirl Creative

Publisher's Cataloging-in-Publication Data
Bennett, John L.
    The essential network : success through personal connections / John L. Bennett. - Mooresville, N.C. : Paw Print Press, c2001

  p. ; cm.
ISBN 0-9678323-1-4

1. Social networks. 2. Business networks. 3. Interpersonal relations. I. Title. II. Success through personal connections

HM741 .B46   2001   2001-93871
302   --dc21   CIP

05 04 03 02 01 5 4 3 2 1

Printed in the United States of America.

To Flip

Acknowledgments

Projects of this magnitude cannot be accomplished without the involvement and support of many people. This project is certainly no exception. While there are hundreds, if not thousands, of people who have touched my life and helped me build a strong network of support, wisdom, and courage, there are a few that will be singled out for recognition. In acknowledging some, I do not mean to minimize anyone's contribution to this work or my life. So, please forgive me in advance for omitting anyone who should be mentioned.

First, this book includes the experiences and knowledge of many people. Some of them are mentioned by name, while others are not. To all of them, my thanks for so generously and rapidly sharing with me in order to benefit others.

Eric Johnson not only encourages me in my work but also supports me in my life. He is the creative and artistic mind (and hands) behind this work–and many other projects. Thank you.

A special "thanks" to Angel Dudley Teer whom I met through networking and who provided editing support to this fast-paced project. You truly are an angel!

Finally, this project would not be possible without the work and support of the people at the Jenkins Group, especially Jerry and Nikki.

Introduction

It has been said, "You are only as strong as your Rolodex." Well, for most of us, a computer and a software program have replaced the Rolodex.

We establish, maintain, and utilize networks in order to build businesses, gain personal comfort and security with others, and develop personally and professionally. Networking is a two-way process. By giving to those in our network, we are more likely to receive from our network. Every networking relationship has at least four beneficiaries: you, your organization, the person with whom you are networking, and his/her organization.

There are diverse benefits of networking. In this book many personal stories illustrate the productive results that can be derived from building connections. These include people who have found their life-partners, avoided personal and financial disasters, made career changes, resolved conflicts, built businesses, met famous people, and more. Entering into a networking relationship with someone can provide many opportunities. Entering into a networking relationship with someone and developing it present responsibilities to the relationship and to the persons involved; however, with those responsibilities come many opportunities.

This book was written in large part by a network of experienced, successful networkers. Use this book as a guide to build and grow your network, to utilize your network more efficiently, and to maintain and cultivate your network more effectively.

Be curious! Ask questions and listen to the answers. People love a good listener who demonstrates genuine interest in them. Use it as a guide to expand your networking skills and strengthen your network whether automated, in a Rolodex, or on index cards.

Believe In Yourself and Your Work

Being self-confident and self-assured is essential to networking, even for the most outgoing individuals.

Think of yourself as a product or resource bank that others need. Approach networking as a way of investing in others. This investment from your resource bank will grow through your connections.

This does require you to know who you are. Believe in your work. Believe in your organization. Believe in yourself. If you don't do these, how can others?

Attend Networking Events

Look for events that will attract the people you want to add to your network. Remember that you are attending the event to meet people more than for the event itself. This may require you to participate in organizations and events that have little interest to you but which attract the people you need to get to know. These events offer rich opportunities to interact with people already in your network. Use networking events to cultivate and enrich existing relationships.

It works...

The greatest benefits I have received from networking include:

a. New ideas

b. Fresh perspectives

c. Reduced stress

d. Genuine friendships/mentorships

e. New skills (especially in mentoring relationships)

f. New job opportunities

g. New insight into perceptions about myself

h. Increased confidence

Michael Rodriguez, manager, American Express Company (Phoenix, AZ)

Prepare Yourself

Do research before going to an event. Find out who will be there and get as much background on them as possible. The more you know the better impression you can make.

When attending networking meetings, ask yourself: What is my reason for attending? What are my goals? What is my plan? How will I execute the plan? How successful was I at each step of the plan? Which follow-up actions are needed?

It works...

I have been privileged to receive invitations to speak, train, write, and preach based on networks. Almost every such opportunity is based on a personal network connection. I've also been able to get special privileges (reduced rates for events, hospitality rooms, free hotel rooms, etc.) for me and for those I know because of networking. Come to think of it, the job I have now came through networking.

Chad Hall, consultant for leadership development and discipleship, Baptist State Convention of North Carolina

Be Punctual

Be on time for every meeting. People notice and make assumptions about your interests and reliability. If you must be late, do it rarely and let the leaders know in advance why you will be late and when they can expect you. Ask the person in charge when would be the best time to arrive late. In some circumstances, it is best to wait until there is a break. For others, joining a group at anytime is appropriate.

Punctuality also means doing what you promise to do, in the manner promised, and within the promised time frame.

It works...

I have gotten concrete leads to contract work as well as the position for which I recently was hired.

Gloria C. Henry, individual and organizational development specialist (Washington, DC)

Dress Appropriately

Dress appropriately for the event: avoid suits at barbecues and shorts at banquets. Make sure your wardrobe is up-to-date and your clothes are well maintained. Buy classic clothes and accessorize with ties, scarves, and pins to show a taste for current fashion trends as appropriate. Unless looking unusual is your business, don't!

It works...

I've gained confidence through my networking. Less than a year ago, I began networking among those who have a strong interest in diversity where I live. Four months later I rarely heard names of people with whom I was not familiar. I'm also confident that I know the latest about what is going on with diversity here in Charlotte. Also, networking has momentum. It's like a snowball effect— the bigger my network is, the more confidence I have, and the larger it grows.

Jennifer Mease, program assistant, Cre8ve Solutions, Inc. (Charlotte, North Carolina)

Make a Positive First Impression

A warm, firm handshake, a smile, an appropriate personal appearance, introducing people to each other, fulfilling promises which have been made, all help to create a positive first impression. Remember that you only get one chance to make a first impression!

It works...

> Networking has given me the edge in competing with other applicants to find and get the job. Specific numbers are quoted, such as salary and commissions, and all are very important when looking for good job fit. Networking has a lot to do with keeping a current business in "tip-top shape". The word gets around that so-and-so is a great spokesperson because that person has taken the trouble to be "interested" in their deal. Anyone who does networking as I do all over the U.S. has to be ready to ask the right things and, most important of all, listen and take those notes.
>
> Pat Davidson, sales manager/pre-construction startup specialist (Charlotte, NC)

Meet People at Events

When attending networking events, whether it is a Chamber of Commerce meeting, a United Way campaign dinner, class, seminar, reunion, or the social hour during a convention, be sure to meet at least five new people. For many, it is easy to isolate themselves by staying only with the people whom they know.

If you are not comfortable walking through a room of strangers and introducing yourself, try one of these three best places to stand in order to meet people at events. One is to stand near the bar or food table. Another option is to stand at the entrance/exit. Everyone goes through the doorway, and almost everyone will go to the bar or food table at least once. Third, if there is a receiving line with dignitaries, stand near it. Everyone wants to meet them. Who knows, maybe you will be associated you with the important people. Besides, this gives you an immediate topic of conversation—the dignitaries.

It works...

My online newsletter has helped create opportunities/invitations to conduct seminars. This free newsletter is now being emailed to friends, colleagues across the country, so the influence has grown.

Edward H. Hammett, leadership consultant, Baptist State Convention of North Carolina

Extend Your Hand

Remember that no one is a stranger once you have introduced yourself. Make eye contact and repeat the person's name several times. Everyone likes hearing one's own name, and you will be more likely to remember it.

If you have any doubt that the other people will recall your name, make it easy for them. Tell them your name and how they might remember you. Don't assume that everyone you remember will remember you.

Practice your handshake so that you are comfortable shaking hands while looking the other person in the eye and talking.

It works...

Networking has helped me successfully move to a new city, effectively change careers, develop long-lasting and meaningful friendships, acquire new clients, and develop a strong referral list for other services. Last but not least, I feel I have made a difference for others with their challenges and needs.

Joan Wright, O'Sullivan Wright Consulting (Charlotte, North Carolina)

Get to Know People Quickly

Quickly locate the people you know at an event and re-introduce yourself to them. They can be your launch pad to meeting others. At each event you attend, introduce yourself to those whom you do not know. This will help you, as well as others, to feel more comfortable in the room. It also adds positive energy. If you wait to be greeted, you may never meet anyone.

Start from the known, and go to the unknown.

It works...

The greatest benefits from networking do not always come from the referrals I receive but from the long-term friendships I've developed. That's more satisfying than any amount of business could ever bring.

Gerri Knilans, president, Trade Press Services (Thousand Oaks, California)

Wear A Nametag

Make sure your name is clearly printed in large bold letters on your nametag. Have a nametag made that incorporates your company name and logo, city/state and boldly displays your name and what you do (e.g., owner, speaker, sales director, vice president for quality, artist, job-seeker). Insert it into a clear plastic nametag holder that you can pick up at most conferences or at an office supply store. Take it with you to every event, just in case one is not provided.

Even if others do not wear nametags at a particular meeting or event, wear yours. This helps others remember your name and helps you standout in the crowd. Frequently, people will introduce themselves and ask where you got your nametag. This is a great way to start a conversation about who they are and their reason for attending the event.

Wear nametags on the right side of your chest. This will make it easier for others to read your name as they shake your hand. Therefore, they will associate your face and your name.

It works...

Networking provides me with more clients, friends, fun, self-confidence, and a higher bottom line. Meeting great friends, gaining support, even staying in the flow of life by socializing and balancing are all benefits.

Ed Primeau, owner, Primeau Productions (Southfield, Michigan)

Embrace New Settings

Put yourself in new networking situations regularly, even if these situations make you feel uncomfortable. Accept invitations to events. It is not necessary to close the party or dinner. Make an appearance.

It works...

My greatest benefit from networking has been my husband—we met through networking. We live in the city and both frequented a local coffee shop. We both were acquaintances with the owner of the coffee shop, and we both were in the middle of house renovations, and the coffee shop owner thought we might want to compare notes. We had seen each other in the coffee shop, but having a formal introduction was more comfortable for us in that setting.

Jennifer Wilson, RN, BSN, neonatal transport nurse, Johns Hopkins Hospital (Baltimore, Maryland)

Talk to Everyone

The person sitting alone or standing in the corner alone may be the person you can help the most and/or will be the key to a gold mine for you. Introduce yourself to everyone.

It is not necessary to engage in long conversations with anyone. Because you are meeting people for the first time, there may be times when you disagree with a point of view. Networking is not the place to disagree vehemently. Learn to disagree gracefully and keep your opinions to yourself until a more appropriate time and place. This requires you to keep an open mind to new ideas and different points of view. Who knows, you may be able to connect two people with the same perspective, thus helping them build their network.

It works...

The greatest benefit I receive from networking is learning what successful people are doing to "manage" the boss or to "manage" the managers or teams or groups of people.

You can gain access to available information through those who are members of various professional organizations. Let's face it - you cannot join them ALL, and the human resources/management sphere encompasses areas that become very specialized. If I have a need for help in information systems, training, quality or benefits, I have access to expert materials through my friends in other professional organizations who can quickly obtain the latest and most correct information. Of course, this means that you must reciprocate when they are in need.

Valerie Pike, SPHR, State of Ohio, Administrative Services, Human Resources Division (Columbus, Ohio)

Be an Attentive Listener

Let the other person speak; you will have time to tell your story when it counts; be patient.

One of the greatest compliments you can give another person is to listen attentively and sincerely. Most people want to tell their story. Listen to them. Ask open-ended questions. Show an interest in what is important to them first and then relate to them from their perspective, not yours.

It works...

I moved to Atlanta three years ago, and I didn't know but one soul in town! I met a wonderful woman at a dinner party. When she heard about the software I had developed, she introduced me to a prominent attorney who specialized in the area of software product development. During a lunch to discuss my software, we began to talk about China. The next week, he introduced me to a professor from Georgia Tech University who had been asked by the Chinese government to assemble an international team of "experts" to inform China of its ecologically sustainable development. I was invited to join the team, and 3 weeks later, I was in Shanghai with a group of world-class environmentalists, educators, artists, and sociologists. None of this would have happened if I hadn't been forthcoming with my interests and experiences.

Dr. Liz Michel, president, Kairos Communicating Strategies, Inc. (Kennesaw, Georgia)

Mix and Mingle

Be one of the last people to take your seat at events. Spend the time meeting others.

Help others get introduced. This takes the attention away from you and helps others get to know one another. You will be remembered as the person who introduced people and who helped them build their network.

It works...

I have moved and lived in a variety of places. My network has assisted me in finding —dentists, mechanics, hairdressers, and personal services from others when I was new in town. It has helped me in finding jobs (helped me avoid disastrous jobs/moves/apartments). And it has helped me to advance in my educational endeavors.

Webra Price Douglas, PhD, CRNP, Maryland Regional Neonatal Transport Program, Johns Hopkins HealthCare (Baltimore, Maryland)

Be Clear and Concise

Be concise and to the point. Learn to communicate effectively and efficiently. Be clear about what you want from others.

It works...

I have learned about other businesses, concepts, and approaches. Networking has allowed me to meet interesting and worthwhile people who usually have mutual interests. There certainly have been opportunities to move into formal as well as informal alliances, discover new business resources, build my credibility, and learn.

James S. Howell, president, BalancedGrowth Solutions, LLC (Mooresville, North Carolina)

Be Visible and Well-liked

People need to see you, know you, and feel comfortable with you. If you make a mistake or believe you may have offended someone, quickly amend the relationship. Don't make another mistake by not addressing it.

Become Knowledgeable

Become knowledgeable about something in such a way that you become a "walking encyclopedia." Read, read, read!

If you are attending an event where many people will have in-depth knowledge of a particular subject (e.g., US Presidents, baseball, golf, postage stamps), do your homework. Know enough to ask a few key questions about the trends of the industry, development of a product, or recent discovery. You shouldn't try to be an expert-just become aware and interested in what is important to them.

Of course, if there is a particular person that you will be meeting, learn about that person. The Internet and the "Who's Who" directories are great resources. Also, your network contacts might be able to help you.

Take a course or workshop. This can be a great way to meet people with at least one common interest. Besides, you might learn something too.

Practice Business Etiquette

There is no substitute for good manners. Get a book about etiquette; read it; practice it. Take a course through a hotel (e.g., Ritz Carlton) or a professional to learn proper etiquette.

As our business and personal lives become more global and less regional, we are required to practice the customs of different cultures. For example, in some settings it is acceptable to eat cornbread crumbled in your soup. It certainly would not be wise to do this at a formal dinner.

Learn the rules and live by them. People will notice.

It works...

> When I moved to the city where I live now, I knew no one but my two cousins and an aunt. I also worked for myself, and my closest client was 150 miles away, so I didn't have the advantage of walking into a big corporation and meeting people every day. The first week I was in town, I asked one of my cousins to go with me to a meeting of a networking/business/social organization I had heard about. There I met a woman who was looking for new blood in an organization with which she was working. I began to volunteer with them and met an entire world of new friends.
>
> Nancy Ring, principal, The Communication Partnership, Ltd. (Charlotte, North Carolina)

Attend Conferences for the BANG

When attending conferences, wear a smile and your nametag, volunteer to introduce panelists, be a greeter, distribute nametags, introduce yourself to speakers and panelists, sit with people you don't know. Carefully choose your sessions, speak up and contribute during workshops and discussions, review the list of attendees and take advantage of the help that everyone there may present. Always be prepared to job-hunt, even if you are not looking for a job.

Attend conferences with a networking agenda. In addition to knowing what you want to accomplish and what you expect to learn, develop goals such as meeting at least five new people with whom you want to develop a relationship. Another goal might be to reconnect with at least five people for "quality, one-on-one time." Prearrange these meetings so that you will not play "chase" during the conference and leave disappointed.

Send speakers and panelists a note about their program. Tell them more about yourself and ask them to put you on their mailing lists.

It works...

Since 1990, I have made NO cold calls or direct mail to market my services. My business has grown double digits every year due to referrals from clients and networking.

Vickie Sullivan, president, Sullivan Speaker Services Inc. (Tempe, Arizona)

Share Conference Materials

When you attend a conference or seminar and you know of others who could benefit but are unable to participate, take along their agendas and bring information, contacts, and materials back for them.

From this, you will participate with a clearer focus. You will help others be successful, and you will also be more likely to meet people that you would not otherwise meet because you are making connections for others. Furthermore, you will have supported some of the people in your network.

It works...

The best part for me is creating some very deep relationships. Some of these people I call just to have a fun conversation. At times, that is all I need from them, and I know they do the same. At other times, I call them when I need some "TLC." They do the same.

Joyce Weiss, MA, CSP, professional speaker (West Bloomfield, Michigan)

Live Beyond the Golden Rule

Do unto others as you would do for yourself. Follow this rule and you will live impeccably and will do the next right thing. This will help you "win friends and influence people."

It works...

Since networking is about establishing contacts and sharing information, it is a process that involves interaction. As a grief counselor and caregiver, it delights me when someone else I'm trying to help benefits from one of my contacts.

John DeBerry, bereavement coordinator, Northwestern Memorial Hospital (Chicago, Illinois)

Brag

Be comfortable bragging about what you have done without being too boastful. Tell your story. Let others know of your accomplishments.

Be a gracious recipient of praise. Accept praise and deflect it to others who are involved in helping you be successful.

Be Impeccable

Build and maintain a positive reputation. Do no wrong. If you do, correct it immediately. Be above reproach.

It works...

I remember an old proverb that says: "To get a friend you must first be a friend." This is the perfect reflection. Instead of trying to make friends by blathering on about yourself at these meetings, go with the thought that you want to make a new friend who will promote you and your business. You do this by shaking hands and asking questions of all your contacts: who and what they are looking for. It doesn't matter what kind of help you offer because it only matters that you help. You will be remembered for a long time because of your free, unsolicited, no payback-expected help.

Mike Stoll, president, The All-Star Agency Speakers Bureau (Fairfax, Virginia)

Be Memorable

Being memorable does not mean wearing a clown suit to a formal dinner.

Tell a funny story or share a memory link for your name. This will help people remember. Send a personal, handwritten note after meeting someone. So few people still send handwritten notes that you are sure to create a favorable impression.

> *It works...*
>
> *I used observational humor every week at our Chamber of Commerce breakfast networking club. It turned me into what I'd call "a minor celebrity"… I became very well—known, and subsequent self-introductions had even more impact as people anticipated a fun introduction! I eventually offered seminars on how to network by developing powerful introductions and had over one hundred people in the chamber attend. Recently, the same seminar was sold out at UNLV. People were turned away, all through the power of networking with a touch of humor.*
>
> John Kinde, humorist (Las Vegas, Nevada)

Learn From Others

Find a networking mentor from whom you can learn. Pay attention to the people who seem to have connections. Especially pay attention to the people you wish to meet. Ask them to help you develop your network. Ask them to tell you how they network. Ask them to allow you to "shadow network" with them.

Relate to Others

Learn to read personalities or thinking styles and use this knowledge to improve your communications and relationships.

Dr. Alan Wolfelt of the Center for Loss and Life Transition in Colorado teaches "companioning". Companioning means to ask others to teach you what they are going through so that you can help them more effectively. Then you can strive not to walk ahead of or behind them, but along side of them.

It works...

My mother went to a local library meeting to hear an author lecture on some topic related to well-being. She told me his information was worthwhile and that I should consult with him. That was nearly 30 years ago. At that point, I was not sure of my life direction. I met the author and one thing led to another. I ended up living on this ranch for four years, working there. In the process, I learned about publishing, running a business as well as media promotion, all of which I use in my current career. I also became best friends with the author's daughter with whom I am still in touch. Who would have thought it?

Andrea H. Gold, president, Gold Stars Speakers Bureau (Tucson, Arizona)

Ask for Permission

Get permission from the person to give his or her name to a new network alliance. Do not randomly and freely give the names of people in your network away. The best connections come when both parties are interested in being introduced. Check this before suggesting one person directly contact another.

Besides, this insures that you have an opportunity to contact the people in your network. It shows that you are protective of the relationship and that you have become associated with the act of connecting two people for the first time.

It works...

I have consistently found that helping other people ALWAYS comes around and benefits my business as well. My consulting business has been built solely through my contacts and referrals from others. Sometimes someone whom I met and helped years ago will refer business to me. I think that in this world which can cause some people to become selfish and focus on their own needs, when you meet someone who is focused on being authentic and really helping others be successful, you remember the favor for a long time. Sincere and helpful people stand out - and are non-threatening - and are the type that others genuinely want to help.

Susan Murphy, PhD, president, Energy Engineering, Inc., co-author of *In the Company of Women: Turning Workplace Conflict into Powerful Alliances* (Houston, Texas)

Ask, Without Questioning

When you meet people for the first time, invest 80% of the conversation in asking them questions about themselves and their business. Talk very little about yourself and your business.

Engage others in conversations. Show curiosity about them, their interests, and their work. However, take great care to avoid questions that make others feel you are interrogating them or getting too personal.

Avoid questions about sex, religion, wages, ex-partners, and politics (unless your are attending a political party function). Only ask questions of others that you would be willing to answer for yourself. Follow this rule and you will avoid embarrassing situations.

Appear Strong

Use a firm (non-aggressive handshake) and good eye contact when you meet someone. Be sure your words and your actions convey assertiveness. Avoid shyness, intimidation, or aggressiveness.

It works...

I think of it as my security blanket! I am not alone in my effort to solve difficult problems, to gather information, to design a program, etc. It can make both your professional and personal lives much more pleasant. I think that it allows your work to be completed in a more efficient manner and at a faster rate. Networking enhances job satisfaction, employee productivity, and customer satisfaction.

Beth Diehl-Svrjcek, RN, MS, NNP, Johns Hopkins HealthCare (Glen Burnie, Maryland)

Find Common Ground

Seek to find common interests and experiences with others. By discovering something in common with others, building a relationship with them becomes much easier.

It works...

Through networking I have gained knowledge, support, and growth. From these come opportunities.

Wanda Craig, W. B. Craig & Associates, Inc. (Charlotte, North Carolina)

Sell Yourself

Know yourself and be able to sell YOU. Offer something people desire. Talk convincingly about the value you offer. Motivate others to speak highly of you and what you have to offer. Deliver more than you promise. Seek ways to add value.

It works...

The most important benefit to me from the networking I have done for the past quarter-century is the friends I have made and the things I have learned from those contacts. On the more tangible basis, I have built a business based on 90% referrals. I have not made a "cold-call" in years and have had a business that has continued to grow and flourish over many years. We have received referrals into many Fortune 100 companies and have even received referrals that resulted in some international travel.

Edward A. Stone, CMC, FIMC, The Dallas Marketing Group, Inc. (Dallas, Texas)

Use an Elevator Statement

Be prepared with a self-introduction. This is your "elevator statement." You should have a 30-second introduction that tells who you are, what you do, whom you work for or represent, and the impact of your work.

Here is an example:
My name is Jane Smith. I create and help others utilize perceptions. As vice president of marketing for a multi-national manufacturing firm, I increased sales and launched five new products. As a leader I used my skills to form, focus, and manage a team of successful professionals...

> **It works...**
>
> I meet people from all over the world. The greatest benefit (and personal reward) I have realized from networking is that I can link people together by explaining how others have coped with similar problems. This is particularly true in developing nations.
>
> Kris A. Karlsen, MSN, RNC, NNP, founder The S.T.A.B.L.E. Program (Park City, Utah)

Distribute Business Cards

Always carry your business card, making sure your business card looks as professional as you care to be remembered. If you are in a virtual business, you may choose to have your photograph printed on your card. This adds a personal touch and helps people relate to you.

Keep the text clean and succinct. Make sure the information is up-to-date and provides appropriate ways for people to contact you. These include mailing and shipping addresses (if different); phone numbers including voice, mobile, and fax; email address; and your website.

Avoid printing a great deal of text about who you are and what you do. Too much text makes cards hard to read and does not allow room for people to write reminders about you and your conversation. Avoid listing more than three contact numbers.

Finally, when collecting the business cards of others, immediately write a note on the back indicating when/where you met, their interests, and one thing you can do to follow up with them within 48 hours.

It works...

I have people in my network that I have consistently networked with for thirty years. One specific individual has been my coach, mentor, advisor, teacher and supporter through some of the most difficult career decisions in my life, including a total career change after twenty years. We have kept each other in touch with new resources, coached each other through leadership issues, and kept each other challenged.
Karen E. Webb, president and CEO, Make-A-Wish Foundation of Central and Western Virginia (Richmond, Virginia)

Learn from Everyone

Talk with people at all levels and from various professions.

Some of the most fascinating conversations you can have are with total strangers. Think about what you can learn from a person willing to share with you who they are while you wait for a plane to arrive or while you sit on a plane for hours. These connections may not immediately or directly build your network, but they can enrich your life by giving you the opportunity to gain the understanding and knowledge that come from relating to others, and thus allowing your network to grow.

It works...

> I have received consulting assignments that went into six figures through contacts with people in my networks. I have found consultants to work with me on assignments. I have expanded the scope of my practice in three major areas through my networks. I have traveled to over 36 countries as a result of these activities. And I have established life-long friendships all over the world with people who have enriched my life.
>
> E. Michael Shays, CMC, FIMC, EMS Consultants (Burlingame, California)

Help Others Introduce You

If you are attending an event as a guest, provide your host with information about yourself that will help to introduce you. Supply your biography, letters of reference, and a sample introductory statement. Make sure that your host receives it in time to review it, to ask questions, and to become comfortable with knowing who you are.

Invite people in your network to join you at social events such as gallery openings, theater events, fund-raising events, professional association meetings, and public seminars. This will help you feel more comfortable with each other and will provide you an opportunity to get better acquainted and to share a common experience. You will also have the opportunity to introduce each other to people attending the event that you did not previously know.

It works...

A coffee meeting with one person led to a one-year contract with a major corporation. The person I met with asked to meet me after we had the opportunity to get to know each other in a professional coaching organization I belonged to.

You may drink gallons of coffee over many months, but it's that one cup that can make the difference (or tea, if you prefer). There's no downside to this. Whether contracts and clients ever come from these sessions, I gain friends and honor my values of connecting, contributing, and creating.

Terry Thirion, personal and professional development coach (Charlotte, North Carolina)

Develop Relationships

Networking is about building lasting relationships with little or no known expectation. When you begin to approach networking with the purpose of getting someone to buy a product or service, you are no longer networking. You are selling. Don't confuse the two.

It works...

I work alone - my network provides me a group of peers I can contact whenever I'm lonely on in need of a shadow consultant or a brainstorming buddy OR...whenever I just need someone to share a cup of coffee with and some good conversation. In four years in Greensboro, through intentional networking efforts, I have come to know more people than I knew previously in South Florida where I lived for 27 years. Networking skills are essential to someone who wishes to go it on their own!

Nancy Probst, Log Cabin Consulting (Greensboro, North Carolina)

Make Referrals Quickly

If you have a business referral for someone, don't wait until the next time you see that person. Share it immediately.

A good rule of thumb is to give at least five times as many referrals to others as you expect in return. Maintain a list of 100 individuals to whom you can refer business as well as those who can refer business to you. Let people know they are on your referral list.

It works...

I have been able to meet and work with leaders in the field. This has helped me find opportunities to be involved in professional activities such as writing and research. Networking has also broadened my area of expertise and sense of community. Furthermore, it has assisted me well in obtaining consultation contracts and referrals.

Katherine M. Jorgensen, RNC, MSN/MBA, Hon.D., KMJ Inc. (Cambridge, Massachusetts)

Ask Everyone for Contacts

Ask for referrals! Each person you meet is a potential hub of connections. Think of all of them as rich resources. Whom do they know that you would like to get to know? Either ask them to introduce you to a particular person, or—ask them if they know someone who may help you with an issue or goal.

Unless others know you well, they cannot refer you. Make sure the people in your network know who you are, how to contact you, what you can do for others, as well as what you need.

It works...

The results include increased business, referral bases, and name recognition. Beyond these standard benefits, I have also been given the opportunity to speak to many organizations and companies about coaching. Some of these opportunities are paid gigs, while others are not. These opportunities give me the benefit of spreading the word about my profession, and they give me the exposure as an expert in the field.

Tracy Stevens, CCC, TLS Associates (Rochester, New York)

Follow Up On All Contacts

Each person you meet is working on a project, raising money for a cause, or dealing with some personal or professional issue. As a good networker, your goal should be to identify the need and help your new contact find a solution.

Identify at least one thing you can do to follow up with all new contacts. This may mean sending them a recent article on a subject of common interest, passing along a greeting to a mutual friend, or connecting them with someone in your network. You can also send them a note saying how pleased you are to have met them.

Use this follow up as a way of reconnecting with the person you have just met and do it within 48 hours.

It works...

Having appropriate contacts in the region has helped my students get good advice and more career opportunities. These connections have also been valuable in my teaching and research to obtain useful information quickly from these sources.

Ruth DeHoog, PhD, political science department, University of North Carolina at Greensboro

Return Phone Calls and E-Mail Promptly

No one likes a person who makes promises and does not follow through. The same is true with phone calls and emails; return them promptly, even if you need to indicate that there will be a delay in fully responding to the people who contact you. This will let them know that you care enough to respond to the message. Ask them for a convenient time to call them back, or ask when they need to hear from you.

It works...

I have gained promotion and support from people that ordinarily would not be a part of my inner-circle.

Daniel Shlifer, Virtual Support Systems (Longboat Key, Florida)

Be a Sponge

Use these basic questions to engage someone:
- *How did you get started in your line of work?*
- *What do you enjoy most about your profession?*
- *What separates you and your company from the competition?*
- *What advice or counsel would you give someone just starting in your business?*
- *What significant changes have you participated in?*
- *What are the coming trends in your business?*
- *Describe the strangest or funniest event you've ever experienced in your business.*
- *What are the most effective ways you've found for promoting your business?*
- *If I were to describe your business to someone else, how would you want me to do that?*
- *Is there anyone here at this event you would like to meet?*

It works...

Through a group of "ambassadors," persons who know the territory and the right people, I have been put in contact with prospects and have had their endorsement of me added to prospects. My ambassadors have been relationship-builder with others therefore significantly reducing the time needed to "break in."

Michael Taylor, marketing director, Berry Sales and Marketing Solutions (Dayton, Ohio)

Congratulate Others

Read daily newspapers and trade publications and send letters of congratulations to people who achieved milestones and deserve admiration. When people in your network have realized a personal or professional success, they have probably worked hard and they deserve to be recognized.

The time to send these notes or cards is as soon as you learn of the accomplishment. Don't worry if your grapevine is slow to get the message to you. Don't be embarrassed if your note is weeks or months after the occasion send it anyway.

The message should be personal and congratulatory. Be specific about the accomplishment and recognize that person for the success that has been achieved.

It works...

On a personal level, networking is having gained the respect of the individuals with whom you work as well as knowing that you have treated those same people as you would like to be treated. On a professional level, it opens numerous opportunities for my organization to participate in activities that probably would not be available otherwise. Networking has brought resources and a positive reputation to the organization that will be here long after I am gone.

Dr. B.J. Reed, dean, College of Public Affairs, University of Nebraska at Omaha

Limit Referrals

Don't give the same referral to more than one or two people in your network. This will wear out your network and dilute your networking power.

It works...

Through networking I obtained my last two jobs, was selected International Association of Business Communicators (IABC) chair, was called upon as a resource by trade publications and often quoted in those publications or asked to speak before communication organizations, and met my best friend!

Brenda C. Siler, director, public relations, American Speech-Language-Hearing Association (ASHA) (Rockville, Maryland)

Consider the Differences

Be cross-culturally aware and sensitive. This means areas including—race, religion, sex, marital status, region of origin, educational level, sexual orientation, religion, etc.

Be sensitive to the differences of others. Carefully "step into their context" and recognize the differences. You can sympathize even when you cannot empathize.

Learn about the cultural differences of others. Be open to experience "their world." Let them disclose to you what they wish–don't pry. Seek to relate to others. Make sure your network is diverse in many ways.

Get Them While They're Hot

Follow up on referrals within 48 hours.

Successful professional speaker and author, David Greenberg, CSP of Atlanta, Georgia says, "I haven't had business cards in nearly three years since I moved to a new address. I collect other people's cards and follow-up with them."

Focus on What's In It For Them

You are probably familiar with the idea of focusing on WII-FM—*What's In It For Me*. In networking, however, the "me" is really "them". So to be successful, you need to stay focused on WII-FT—*What's In It For THEM*. Always consider what you can do for others. Try to imagine their needs and their desires first.

Pay close attention to the needs, desires, and interest of individuals in your network. Continuously think in terms of what you can do for them. The payback will come. Be patient. Be focused on other people.

Be Patient

Networking takes time and hard work. Creating a network of people that you can call upon or to whom you can refer others can only be done one relationship at a time.

Continuously assess whether a person you are working to add to your network is interested in being a part of your connection tree. Don't be too pushy yet be persistent. And, above all, be patient. A good relationship takes time to develop; it is worth the wait.

It works...

Strong relationships develop with really great people, some of whom have become clients.

Michael Claggett, CMC, president, Anderson Claggett Consulting (New York, New York)

Be the "dots"

Constantly seek to understand the needs of others and link them with people in your network who have a solution. Sometimes the people in your network are not the immediate solution to another person's need, but through their network they can find a solution.

Ask people in your network whom they want to meet. Help them by taking them to lunch or coffee or by introducing them at a networking event. Create a hub around which other networks are connected.

Keep Others Informed

Keep people in your network informed of your work and your accomplishments. When you receive an award or a promotion, change jobs, or obtain a level of distinction in your profession, send a press release to professional associations for which you are a member, the local business media, and your clients, prospects, and network. By keeping them informed, you will get the exposure that you want, and will help others get to know you better.

Be sure to send change of address changes when you move.

It works...

Networking has provided me with opportunities to meet people who are redefining the leading edge of my field. A few months ago I attended an event for the sole purpose of networking. As luck would have it, I ended up at a table with a former Fortune 500 VP who is doing Ph.D. research on factors that shape a CEO's leadership style. This is a particular interest of mine, we have maintained contact, and I will be introducing her to colleagues who are interested in her work as well. We both win!

Nancy Kuhn, Organizational Learning (Alexandria, Virginia)

Use Technology

Keep your personal data assistant (PDA) up-to-date and with you at all times; it's your lifeline. Be sure to carry extra batteries or a recharging cord.

Make certain that your PDA and your primary database (if not the same) are synchronized on a regular basis.

Cell phones are also a terrific tool to help you stay in touch. Keep a list of network contacts to call while waiting for a bus, train, or plane-or even between appointments. Use email to send quick notes and forward articles. It's fast and convenient.

It works...

> The greatest benefits of networking have come in starting a charitable organization. In 1994 I asked some like-minded women if they were interested in helping needy children to get new back-to-school clothing and shoes. A small group came together to brainstorm ideas. "Send'em Off Smiling" was registered as a charitable organization in 1998 and this year has a Board of 10 Directors and will help 750 children.
>
> Jill Malleck, senior human resources consultant, Manulife Financial (Waterloo, Ontario, Canada)

Use the Power of Your Database

Use an automated database management system. There are many excellent electronic databases on the market that can easily be learned.

Learn to use the database system to your advantage. Make notes of spouses and children, personal and professional interests. Also make note of the last time you had contact with the person. Create a way to sort your database to locate members of your network. In most database programs you can create customized identification codes.

Make sure you maintain a backup of your database file. Keep it off-site. That means not having it in the office if your system is at work, not having it at home if your database is at home. Periodically purge the database. Not everyone you meet will become a part of your network. You be the judge for deleting them. Is it after not-reciprocal contact in six months or two years? Keep the business cards you collect so that you still have the contacts long after you have deleted them from your active network list. These cards can serve as an additional backup file—just in case.

It works...

One person in my network is a professional fundraiser. On one occasion I was able to contract her to work on a short-term project for me when I had a staff person leave in the middle of a critical client proposal season. This was not a job that a normal consultant would have accepted, but because of my continued relationship with her, she agreed to help me out.

Patricia D'Alba, CFRE, vice president, Grizzard (Atlanta, Georgia)

Participate in Mastermind Groups

Mastermind groups are more than a networking group. They are people who meet regularly to challenge and support each other professionally. In addition to the brainpower of four to six other individuals, you gain access to their networks. These groups provide a terrific way to support your professional and business development while expanding your network.

It works...

Comradeship, talking to others in related fields, sharing ideas and discussing new techniques are just a few of the benefits I have gained through networking. The ability to call on one another for ideas or help in a difficult situation has helped me tremendously.

Malvern D. Lusky, L-Factor (Sugar Land, TX)

Collect and Send Articles and Clippings

Using your network database, make a note of the interests of others. Clip articles for them and mail them with a short note.

For example: "I know _____ is of interest to you. Thought you might enjoy this article. Best regards..."

It works...

Herman Cain, chairman of Godfather's, nominated me for the Horatio Alger Award because the woman who helps him with his intellectual property rights and promotions was in two women's groups I had started. One of my sponsors for the nomination was Mark Victor Hansen, author of Chicken Soup for the Soul, *etc. whom I was introduced to by Somers White. Somers is the champion of networking.*

Cella Quinn, Cella Quinn Investment Services (Omaha, Nebraska)

Mail Business Cards

Include your business card with all correspondence, including bill payments. These inexpensive mini-ads should be given away. Who knows where the mail clerk may put them? By inserting them into your correspondence, you are spreading your name and reminding people who you are.

Send Greeting Cards

Some people have found that sending Thanksgiving cards is more effective than sending Christmas cards because not everyone celebrates Christmas. Your gesture of kindness will signal you as a thoughtful, caring person. Be sure to write a personal note on each card. Never use a preprinted signature. Sending cards at various holidays gives you an opportunity to stay in contact with members of your network.

Use your network database to remind you of birthdays and anniversaries. Send greetings and best wishes. By staying in touch with your network, you will know about illnesses, births, and deaths. Use these occasions as opportunities to send cards and notes. Flowers, books, and food are also good to send.

Send Quick Notes

Carry thank-you notes with you so that you can write quick notes after you meet someone. Promptly writing a courtesy note or a thank-you note will create a lasting positive impression of you on the receiver.

Use your network database to track the people you have not talked with, seen or corresponded with in several months. Send them a brief note to let them know that you are thinking of them. Ask about something of interest to them. Mention a recent accomplishment (yours as well as theirs).

Hire a professional graphic designer to create personal note cards for you.

It works...

First and last, networking provides me with the gift of friends and the opportunity to serve. I force myself not to think of what I am receiving because that appeals to the lower part of my nature and intentions. If I, however, look for goodness and attempt to shed light on it, all becomes well, and I receive in ways that cannot be measured but that are indeed very real and meaningful.

Pat Morand, general manager, Aventis Bio-Services (Northbrook, Illinois)

Send Thank-you Notes

If you don't get a contract or a job, or close a sale, send the person a thank-you note anyway. This will position you as a gracious person. Thank that person for taking time to meet with you and to consider you and/or your proposal.

Who knows, your services might be needed in the future. Leave that person with a positive impression. Leave a positive impression by getting your name and business card in the hands of that person one more time.

Go Prospect Mining

Contact the alumni office of colleges and universities you attended. Ask for a directory of your classmates. The same is true for high school classmates. Identify those you know (even slightly) and whom you would like to add to your network. Contact them; rekindle a friendship.

Get the list of conference, seminar, or convention attendees. Review the list and contact the people you met or had hoped to meet during the course of the meeting. Send them a note reflecting on having met them or wishing that you had had the opportunity to do so. Develop a friendship.

Encourage Others

Encourage others to reach their dreams and goals. By helping others achieve their goals, you will get to know them better, possibly use your network to help them, and create an endearing "networkship" (that's a friend in your network). The payoff will come through the success of others.

Schedule Time

Allocate time to make phone calls and write notes to people in your network. Schedule yourself time to attend as many activities as possible. By doing so you will build and maintain your network. Fill your schedule with events that put you in front of the people you wish to meet.

Play golf or tennis at a time when you are likely to meet others. Join a health club attended by the people you wish to meet. Learn when they workout and do the same.

Be a Host

It is easy to fall into the role of "guest" when you meet others. Be a "host" by starting conversations, introducing others, and making sure the needs of others are met.

It works...

When I was a young professional in Dallas, I joined an area Chamber of Commerce's public relations committee that met at 6:30 am! However, the interaction with those professionals was very rewarding, and as a young college graduate, it gave me the confidence to know that my ideas, skills, and passion were as strong as anyone else's were.

Dr. Gene C. Crume, vice president for Institutional Advancement, Mars Hill College (Mars Hill, North Carolina)

Volunteer

By getting involved as a volunteer in professional associations, civic groups, church activities and community agencies, you will have the opportunity to meet many people. These organizations provide excellent opportunities to showcase your skills and talents.

Serve on one to four committees or boards of directors, but never more than that. Avoid spreading yourself too thin. Be an active member.

Volunteer to serve on the nominating committee of volunteer organizations. This will provide you with the opportunity to work with the organization's leaders and to gain exposure to those being considered for the board. You may have the opportunity to recruit others to join the organization in a prestigious leadership role.

Volunteer to speak at professional and business organizations. Give your time and your talents away. Write articles for newsletters.

Don't be a "grandstand member" of organizations; don't be a "bench-sitter"; be an actively engaged, vital participant.

It works...

Volunteer your expertise to groups, clubs, and not-for-profit organizations. By being involved within one of my volunteer boards, we were able to bring a significant piece of convention business to the area that amounted to over $500,000 in economic impact to the community. Networking has also put me in contact with several business leaders in our community with whom I am now on a first-name basis, and I know whom to call if I need something done.
Tom Galyon, president/CEO, Greater Lansing Convention & Visitors Bureau (Lansing, Michigan)

Be a Mentor

By becoming a mentor to others, you will help them grow and develop. You will help mold them into a good networker. This may come back to support you in the future.

By being a mentor, you are able to connect the person who is being mentored with people in your network. This will connection support both parties.

> *It works...*
>
> *I obtained one of the best and greatest mentors that anyone could ask for by forwarding a thank-you note. She gave me endless information and assistance as I began my speaking career.*
> Eileen O. Brownell, professional speaker/author/coach, Training Solutions (Chico, California)

Hire a Coach

Work with a professional coach to support you in your networking skill development. Believe it or not, there are professionally trained and certified coaches who specialize in helping people build, maintain, and utilize their networks. If you can't find a friend or person in your network to serve as a mentor, hire a professional coach.

It works...

Assertive networking has brought us clients, good friends, a wide range of opportunities to travel, ways to engage in joint business ventures, and important quality growth for our network.

Roger Herman and Joyce Gioia, consultants and futurists, The Herman Group (Greensboro, North Carolina)

Continuously Learn

Continuously seek to learn from your networking experiences.

Networking has been an integral part of being effective and efficient in business and in life for a long time. Building, maintaining, and improving your network and your networking skills are keys to success. It is a constant and evolving process.

Identify people for your network who are excellent at networking. Add them to your network and learn from them. What events do they attend? Whom do they know? How do they handle themselves? How do they support others?

It works...

In 1997 I took the reins of a small boutique consulting and training practice on the wane, and I used my accumulated network of contacts and previous clients as the starting place to spread the word of my new venture and brand. I built a website designed to nurture a network of best-practitioners. I created an e-newsletter that would keep providing value to that network (growing from 2000 people on my list to over 20,000 in two years). I was able to get my book published by directly mining that network for the resources I needed. Hanging out and conversing with a friend who had been in the publishing business turned me on to my agent who used her network to connect me with a terrific editor and publisher. All the best things that have ever happened to me can be traced to my willingness to risk meeting and engaging with someone whom I didn't know previously, and my network provided every one of those opportunities.

David Allen, founder and president, David Allen Company, author, *Getting Things Done: the Art of Stress-Free Productivity* (Oiai, California)

11 Principles of Networking for Success

1) Seek to understand others before you seek to have them understand you.

2) Build relationships; the network will follow.

3) Generously share your network with others.

4) Be yourself; be authentic; be confident.

5) Treasure your network as you would a delicate possession that needs care and attention.

6) Be prepared to tell others about yourself.

7) Recognize others; don't be afraid to say "Thank You."

8) Be trustworthy; earn and give respect.

9) What you give will be returned—be generous to others.

10) Continuously learn to improve your networking skills.

11) Delight in knowing people.

Bibliography and Resources

Baker, Wayne E. *Networking Smart: How to Build Relationships for Personal and Organizational Success,* New York: McGraw-Hill, 1994.

Burg, Bob. *Endless Referrals,* New York: McGraw-Hill, 1998.

Carnegie, Dale, et al. *How to Win Friends and Influence People,* Pocket Books.

Fisher, Donna and Sandy Vilas. *Power Networking Second Edition: 59 Secrets for Personal and Professional Success,* Austin: Mountain Harbor Publications, 1992.

Leeds, Dorothy. *Smart Questions: A New Strategy for Successful Managers,* New York: Berkley Books, 1987.

Mackay, Harvey. *Dig Your Well Before You're Thirsty,* New York: Currency, 1997.

Misner, Ivan R. *7 Second Marketing: How to Use Memory Hooks to Make You Instantly Stand Out in a Crowd,* Atlanta: Bard Press, 1996.

Misner, Ivan R. and Don Morgan. *Masters of Networking: Building Relationships for Your Pocketbook and Soul,* Atlanta: Bard Press, 2000.

About the Author

John Bennett, MPA, CMC is president of Lawton & Associates, an international organizational development consulting firm that specializes in helping individuals and organizations prepare for, excel through, and improve from change. He is a consultant, executive coach, speaker/trainer and author of numerous articles. He is also the author of *Leading the Edge of Change*.

He lives on Lake Norman, near Charlotte, North Carolina, and travels extensively working with domestic and international clients.

John Bennett can be reached for keynote speeches, seminars, consulting, and executive coaching through:

Lawton & Associates
1 (877) 8LAWTON
www.lawton-assoc.com

ORDER FORM

The Essential Network
Success Through Personal Connections

1–50 copies	___ copies at $8.95 each
51–99 copies	___ copies at $7.95 each
100–300 copies	___ copies at $6.95 each
301 or more copies	___ copies at $6.00 each

Name _____
Title _____
Organization _____
Phone (_____) _____
Shipping Address _____
City _____ State/Province _____
Postal Code _____ Country _____
Email Address _____

Applicable sales tax, shipping and handling charges will be added.
Prices subject to change.

❑ Check Enclosed   ❑ VISA   ❑ MASTERCARD

Account Number _____ Expiration Date _____
Signature _____

To order, call (704) 660-6000 or fax to (704) 660-9631.
Email: books@lawton-assoc.com
or mail this form to:
    P.O. Box 3816
    Mooresville, NC 28117